P9-CDI-611

ALSO BY CALViN TRiLLiN

FEEDING A YEN

TEPPER ISN'T GOING OUT

FAMILY MAN

MESSAGES FROM MY FATHER

TOO SOON TO TELL

DEADLINE POET

REMEMBERING DENNY

AMERICAN STORIES

ENOUGH'S ENOUGH

TRAVELS WITH ALICE

IF YOU CAN'T SAY SOMETHING NICE

WITH ALL DISRESPECT

KILLINGS

THIRD HELPINGS

UNCIVIL LIBERTIES

FLOATER

ALICE, LET'S EAT

RUNESTRUCK

AMERICAN FRIED

U.S. JOURNAL

BARNETT FRUMMER IS AN UNBLOOMED FLOWER

AN EDUCATION IN GEORGIA

OBLIVIOUSLY ON
HE SAILS

OBLiViOUSLY ON HE SAiLS

The Bush Administration in Rhyme

CALViN TRiLLiN

RANDOM HOUSE NEW YORK

Discard
NHCPL

NEW HANOVER COUNTY
PUBLIC LIBRARY
201 CHESTNUT STREET
WILMINGTON, NC 28401

Copyright © 2004 by Calvin Trillin

All rights reserved under International and Pan-American Copyright Conventions.
Published in the United States by Random House, an imprint of The Random House
Publishing Group, a division of Random House, Inc., New York, and simultaneously in
Canada by Random House of Canada Limited, Toronto.

RANDOM HOUSE and colophon are registered trademarks of Random House, Inc.

LIBRARY OF CONGRESS CATALOGING-IN-PUBLICATION DATA
Trillin, Calvin.
Obliviously on he sails : the Bush administration in rhyme / by Calvin Trillin.
    p.   cm.
ISBN 1-4000-6288-8
1. Bush, George W. (George Walker), 1946– Poetry.   2. United States—Politics
and government—2001– Poetry.   3. Republican Party (U.S. : 1854–)—Poetry.
4. Presidents—United States—Poetry.   5. Political poetry, American.   I. Title.
PS3570.R5O25 2004
811'.54—dc22   2004045052

The poems in this book originally appeared in *The Nation*. Some passages in the
text first appeared in *Time* or *The New Yorker*.

Printed in the United States of America on acid-free paper

Random House website address: www.atrandom.com

9 8 7 6 5 4 3

Book design by Casey Hampton

TO ABIGAIL TRILLIN AND SARAH STEWART TRILLIN

A father who finds himself with two Cordelias can count his blessings.

CONTENTS

Part 1

GEORGE W. BUSH AND
NANNY DICK

THE EFFECT ON HiS CAMPAiGN OF THE RELEASE OF GEORGE W. BUSH'S COLLEGE TRANSCRiPT

Obliviously on he sails,
With marks not quite as good as Quayle's.

—NOVEMBER 29, 1999

he fact that those marks at Yale got him into Harvard Business School is yet another reminder of which class of Americans has always benefited from the original affirmative action program. When George W. Bush began to be spoken of as a possible presidential candidate, he had to counter a widespread impression that he was just a shallow rich boy who had failed at everything except riding along on family connections. Given what Bush's college transcript revealed, it occurred to me that Dick Cheney, who flunked out of Yale twice, might have been put on the ticket because he was the only living American politician who had a less distinguished academic record at Yale than George W. Bush.

The theory prevalent among more responsible observers was that Cheney, who had been in charge of finding the Republican vice-presidential nominee, selected himself as a sort of nanny to the relatively inexperienced Bush. I have always thought of Cheney as The Droner. His greatest talent has been to create a public persona that makes him appear to be, despite his congressional voting record and his views, too boring to be extreme.

In the past, I'd suggested campaign slogans to candidates of both parties—sometimes the same slogan, as in the tried-and-true "Never Been Indicted." In that spirit, I offered Bush a campaign slogan that I'd once offered Quayle, a student of similar limitations who was in the DePauw chapter of Bush's college fraternity, Delta Kappa Epsilon: "Definitely Not the Dumbest Guy in the Deke House." The offer was not accepted.

A SCIENTIFIC OBSERVATION ON THE SPEAKING PROBLEMS THAT SEEM TO RUN IN THE BUSH FAMILY

He thinks that *hostile*'s *hostage*.
He cannot say *subliminal.*
The way Bush treats the language
Is bordering on criminal.

His daddy had the problem:
He used the nounless predicate.
Those cowboy boots can do that
To people from Connecticut.

—OCTOBER 9, 2000

ON THE WHITE HOUSE DRESS CODE

The President's demanding proper dress—
A tie, a coat, a shine on shoes or boots.
I guess we're meant to find this a relief:
We've now returned to government by suits.

—APRIL 2, 2001

DICK CHENEY'S PRIMER ON THE CONSTITUTION

So what's it called if during war you criticize the President for
  any reason?
Treason.
And how long does this war go on (and this is where this
  theory's really pretty clever)?
Forever.

—JUNE 10, 2002

CHENEY'S HEAD: AN EXPLANATION

One mystery I've tried to disentangle:
Why Cheney's head is always at an angle.
He tries to come on straight, and yet I can't
Help notice that his head is at a slant.
When Cheney's questioned on the Sunday shows,
The Voice of Reason is his favorite pose.
He drones in monotones. He never smiles—
Explaining why some suspects don't need trials,
Or why right now it simply stands to reason
That criticizing Bush amounts to treason,
Or which important precept it would spoil
To know who wrote our policy on oil,
Or why as CEO he wouldn't know
What Halliburton's books were meant to show.
And as he speaks I've kept a careful check
On when his head's held crooked on his neck.
The code is broken, after years of trying:
He only cocks his head when he is lying.

—JUNE 24, 2002

A SHORT HISTORY OF DICK CHENEY AS MINDER

At first, we thought we should be glad
To have a nanny for the lad—
Young Bush, who might be overawed,
Who'd barely even been abroad,
Who seemed to us a lightweight laddie
Who'd need a sitter sent by daddy.

But Cheney's shop became the place
Where fantasists would make their case:
Iraqis threaten. At the least,
We'd rearrange the Middle East
And rule the world forevermore
If we just smashed them in a war.

Dick bought this bunk, and sold it, too.
He lied back then, and he's not through.
He'd fooled the rubes like you and me
Who never thought that he would be
A zealot once he got installed.
Stealth Nanny's what he should be called.

—DECEMBER 8, 2003

I'M AN OLD COWHAND, AS SUNG BY GEORGE W. BUSH

(With apologies to Johnny Mercer)

I'm an old cowhand from the hinterland,
Which an Eastern wuss wouldn't understand.
Ain't a rich folks' tax cut I wouldn't sign,
But I don't know no one who drinks white wine.
How 'bout Kenneth Lay? Weren't no friend of mine.
Yippee i oh ti-ay! Yippee i oh ti-ay!

I'm a cowpoke, folks. Don't eat artichokes.
Burgers do me fine. Wash 'em down with Cokes.
In my battle flight suit I'll strike a pose,
But I got compassion, down to my toes.
It's for unborn babies and CEOs.
Yippee i oh ti-ay! Yippee i oh ti-ay!

I'm a cowboy, guys. This is no disguise.
I don't flip or flop. I don't agonize.
Ain't no bad guy goin' I won't bombard.
Kerry's soft on bad guys and I am hard—
Toughest hombre ever hid in the Guard.
Yippee i oh ti-ay! Yippee i oh ti-ay!

—APRIL 5, 2004

Part 2

JESUS AND MAMMON TEAM UP TO SEE GEORGE W. BUSH THROUGH THE PRIMARIES

ON THE LATEST REPUBLICAN DEBATE

I watched these presidential hopefuls join
Together for debating in Des Moines,
And many times I heard allegiance sworn
To Jesus and to babies not quite born.
At times, this thought occurred to me: I hope
They don't think what they're running for is pope.

—JANUARY 3, 2000

*E*arly in the 2000 primary campaign, I noticed a remarkable coincidence: In the entire country, there were only three rich, high-born Episcopalians who were fervently antiabortion, and every one of them was running for the Republican presidential nomination.

One of the candidates was Steve Forbes, whose hunt-country neighbors had never been moved to block access to abortion clinics with their fox hounds. The second was George W. Bush, who had been brought to Jesus (on the way to Methodism) by Billy Graham, the only American evangelist whose notion of hell is a place where he doesn't get to play golf with the President. The third was John McCain.

Bush's huge campaign war chest made him a strong favorite. Then McCain trounced him in New Hampshire. In the South Carolina primary, a must-win for the survival of the Bush candidacy, rumors cropped up about McCain—about his mental state, about his family. It was whispered that McCain's years as a prisoner of the North Vietnamese had made him unstable. George W. Bush had fulfilled his military obligations in the Texas Air National Guard—although for a year or so he apparently hadn't felt obligated to attend the required meetings. Bush had benefited from the sort of influence Colin Powell presumably had in mind when he wrote, in *My American Journey,* "I am angry that so many sons of the powerful and well placed . . . managed to wrangle slots in Reserve and National Guard units." There were no rumors about George W. Bush's "temperament." Why would anyone question the stability of someone rational enough to avoid a place where people might shoot at him?

THE WRECK OF THE PRIMARY CAMPAIGN
(A Republican Sea Chantey)

They boned up on the issues, like
Abortion and the flag.
Republicans were running hard,
Then they began to sag.
For Bush had gathered campaign funds
In staggering amounts.
Yes, Bush has got the money, lads,
And money's all that counts.

Yes, Bush has got the money, lads.
The others are in tatters.
The Shrub has got the do-re-mi
And money's all that matters.

The lobbyists gave right away.
As business this was sound.
They think they see a winner, and
The floor they want is ground.
That's why the race is all but done.
That's why no tension mounts.
'Cause Bush has got the money, lads,
And money's all that counts.

—JULY 26, 1999

WELCOME, MALCOLM S. FORBES, JR.

And now we have a junior Forbes,
Named Steve, who cheerfully absorbs
The campaign costs. (For he enjoys
What daddy couldn't spend on toys.)
He longs for tax rates that are flat—
The same for him, a plutocrat,
As for his gardeners and his chars
And all the men who wax his cars.
Economies, he says, can grow
If builders get to keep their dough.
If all of them are forced to share it,
They'll lose incentive to inherit.

—NOVEMBER 13, 1995

FAREWELL, STEVE FORBES

We mutter adieu now to Steve,
Who finally decided to leave.
We thought he might never be done
With buying his place in the sun.

So is there some lesson in why
His gilt-edged campaign failed to fly?
The theories that pundits now share
Are nuanced, and full of hot air.

So now they can listen to mine:
To paraphrase old Gertrude Stein,
Though Forbes could give barrels of pork,
A dork is a dork is a dork.

—MARCH 6, 2000

ORRIN HATCH ENDS WHATEVER IT WAS

The Orrin Hatch campaign is done—
Kaput at last, without a doubt.
And now, perhaps, could someone please
Explain what that was all about?

—FEBRUARY 21, 2000

ENTER MRS. DOLE

Elizabeth Dole is all perfection.
She shoots one take, without exception.
She drives her staff so no step's spared
To get an ad-libbed speech prepared.
There's not a wrinkle in her dress.
Her hairdo makes Lott's look a mess.
So will some human adversary
Say Mrs. Dole is sort of scary?

—APRIL 5, 1999

A FAMILY-DYNAMICS ANALYSIS OF ELIZABETH DOLE'S WITHDRAWAL

Though Bob has said he's giddy over Liddy,
He didn't do a lot to help her, did he.

—NOVEMBER 15, 1999

MCCAIN

So now comes forward John McCain—
A high-tech version of Gawain
When with his steed, a Navy plane.
He says he's forming his campaign
Committee, which will ascertain
If someone known for speaking plain
And taking stands that are the bane
Of those protecting their domain
With campaign cash that they obtain
From fat cats who might then ordain
In laws some clauses that pertain
To only those whose favors gain
The sort of access that's germane
Can, in a party whose disdain
For folks who go against the grain
Has caused reformers only pain,
Be nominated to regain
The White House for a four-year reign.
Or, as the experts all maintain,
Does John McCain campaign in vain?

—JANUARY 25, 1999

ADMIRATION FROM AFAR

They like the way he's not afraid to say
That money lets the fat cats get their way.
They like his style, the fact he doesn't pander.
They like it when he demonstrates his candor
By skewering his party with a zinger.
Alas for him, McCain's the left's right-winger.

—NOVEMBER 22, 1999

THE MESSAGE OF THOSE SPREADING RUMORS
ABOUT JOHN MCCAIN'S "TEMPERAMENT"

Imprisonment and torture are the sort
Of things that might just drive a person daft.
So just in case that happened to McCain,
Let's stick with candidates who dodged the draft.

—DECEMBER 13, 1999

A THEOLOGICAL ANALYSIS OF THE SOUTH CAROLINA PRIMARY

In Greenwich, the land of the Bushes,
The men of the cloth all wore tweed.
And one didn't meet any Christians
Like Robertson, Falwell, and Reed.

But politics calls for adjustments.
If right is the wing that you need,
You praise God and shout Hallelujah
With Robertson, Falwell, and Reed.

So Bush, the uniter from Texas,
Said, "Since you're the fellows they heed,
Do Jesus's work down and dirty,
Please, Robertson, Falwell, and Reed."

They blackened McCain with their phone banks,
And told all the voters that he'd
Consort with the people most hated
By Robertson, Falwell, and Reed.

McCain's just too chummy with Satan,
And should he, not Bush II, succeed,
The unborn would have no protector,
Said Robertson, Falwell, and Reed.

Well, W won Carolina.
For three days he had back his lead.
For this he had pledged his allegiance
To Robertson, Falwell, and Reed.

Yes, he made his pact—not with Satan,
But, still, he will never be freed.
He'll always be part of a package
With Robertson, Falwell, and Reed.

—MARCH 13, 2000

A ROBERTSON REPUBLICAN
(A Gilbert and Sullivan Solo for George W. Bush)

Though folks in Texas are diverse, I knew I could unite them all.
Endorsements came from blacks and girls; I'd happily recite
    them all.
I've sympathy for everyone (I bleed a lot for Texaco).
I really can't be prejudiced: my sister-in-law's from Mexico.
Though I was real compassionate—at least that is the tale we
    spun—
I am, when all is said and done, a Robertson Republican.

CHORUS:
He is, when all is said and done, a Robertson Republican.

I needed Pat to smear McCain as baby killer and profane,
Or smite him with a hurricane, so I could win this one
    campaign.
And Falwell, too, was fine, I felt. So I, to smash my rival, dealt
With guys who really raise a welt with cheap shots from the
    Bible Belt.
I am a onetime lapdog's son, so it may not strike anyone
As odd that I'm content to run as one who's to the left of
    none—a Robertson Republican.

He is a onetime lapdog's son, so it may not strike anyone
As odd that he's content to run as one who's to the left of
  none—a Robertson Republican.

—MARCH 27, 2000

LET'S HEAVE HO TOWARD THE CENTER, LADS
(Another Republican Sea Chantey)

Let's heave ho toward the center, lads.
Don't show the world the right.
Let's heave ho toward the center, lads
Keep Falwell out of sight.

Let's heave ho toward the center, lads.
To win we must be willing
To cool it on abortion, so
Don't speak of baby killing.

Let's heave ho toward the center, lads.
The center's all the rage.
Whatever blacks we have, lads,
We'll line up on the stage.

Let's heave ho toward the center, lads.
We think the folks will buy it.
So bigots hold your tongues, please.
Meshuggeners, be quiet.

—AUGUST 21, 2000

Part 3

THE JESUS-MAMMON TEAM TRIUMPHS, THANKS TO A LAST-MINUTE FIVE-POINTER BY THE SUPREME COURT

WHEREFORE AL GORE?

They're asking now, "Wherefore Al Gore?"
They're thinking now, "Should we explore
A few alternatives before
We find too late we've bet the store
And stuck ourselves forevermore
With someone whom we don't abhor
But find—well, though with gifts galore
And talents that we can't ignore
And children we could all adore
And, so we're told, a great rapport
With folks in smallish groups, say four
Or three or maybe two—a bore?"

And late at night they ask themselves, quite madly,
"You think it's just too late to get Bill Bradley?"

—MAY 10, 1999

*a*nd so this New World meritocracy held a presidential race between the son of President George H. W. Bush and the son of Senator Albert Gore, Sr. If they hadn't been candidates by inheritance, how would they have presented themselves for the first political offices they'd won? George W. Bush's pitch might have been, "I was a mediocre student at Yale, and then, after knocking around for a while, I finally made some money on a deal I got into through my family connections, and I'd make you a real good governor." Al Gore, whom I'd once described as a "manlike object," could have said, "I was a mediocre student at Harvard, and I have an almost stupefying inability to make contact with other human beings, so I think I should be your congressman."

How did the Bush dynasty last long enough to serve up George W. Bush? In 1980, his father, the patriarch of a family identified for years with Planned Parenthood, declared himself an opponent of abortion in order to become Ronald Reagan's running mate. Imagine lunch at Kennebunkport the next day:

"Guys," George H. W. says to his grown sons, "as it turns out, abortion is not a matter of a woman's right to control of her own body after all. It's baby killing, pure and simple."

"Fine, Pop," Jeb says. "Sounds good. Baby killing it is."

"Okay, Pop," George W. Bush says. "Whatever. Can I use the boat this afternoon?"

George H. W. Bush turns to look seriously at his wife. "Bar," he says, "I believe this is the best apple cobbler I've ever put in my mouth."

SECOND THOUGHTS

So what was the matter with Kasich?
And what was so bad about Dole?
And why did we sour on poor Gary Bauer
And find naught in Hatch to extol?

And what was the problem with Gephardt?
And why did we seem to ignore
The Democrats who, at least in their view,
Were credible options to Gore?

With options now gone for both parties,
The winners don't hold us in thrall.
We're now sighing sighs that these are the guys
We're stuck with for good in the fall.

—APRIL 10, 2000

ONE DAY iN THE LiFE OF THE PALM BEACH COUNTY RECOUNT

While Bush says counting votes by hand's unfair,
Gore gains—a *bubbe* here, a *zayde* there.

—DECEMBER 4, 2000

i'M COUNTiNG MY HEART OUT FOR YOU
(Lyrics Found on a Table inside a State
Building in Miami-Dade County)

I'm counting my heart out for you.
The votes I am finding are few.
We hear the mob right in the hallway heat up;
They're talking of the chads that we might eat up.
I hope this ends before we all get beat up.
I'm looking for voters for you—
Some blacks or a wandering Jew.
There aren't enough new hanging chads to suit me.
I hope the Cubans don't show up to shoot me.
There doesn't seem much I can do,
Still, I'm counting my heart out for you.

—DECEMBER 18, 2000

A SURVEY OFFERING DEMOCRATS TWO RESPONSES
TO THE RETURN OF AL GORE TWO YEARS AFTER HIS DEFEAT

Al Gore is back:
   (1) Alas
   (2) Alack

—MAY 6, 2002

ON NOT RUNNING FOR THE PRESIDENCY

We now feel warm toward Albert Gore,
Who will not run in aughty-four.
Most candidates, I must admit,
Seem at their best the day they quit.

—JANUARY 13, 2003

Part 4

THE SUPPORTING CAST
ENTERS FROM STAGE RiGHT

SiLVER LiNiNGS

I

Now Ashcroft will decide who's on the bench.
The Civil Rights Division will retrench—
Unless it finds that civil rights entails
Some breaks at last for pure white Christian males.
The jobs and housing efforts that depend
On Justice will on Ashcroft's watch all end.
And solemn friend-of-court briefs will be filed:
"Abortion simply means to kill a child."
One comfort lasts, as dreams of justice shatter:
Ralph Nader said it really wouldn't matter.

II

Gale Norton thinks there's no place you can spoil
If what you do to it produces oil.
She'd like to see no regulations left;
She thinks controls on property is theft.
Emissions? Who should monitor their flow?
To her it's clear: the firm's own CEO.
So drillers drill. Here's what Interior's got:
A protégée of James (The Crackpot) Watt.
Don't tear your hair and curse those who begat her.
Remember: Nader said it wouldn't matter.

—JANUARY 22, 2001

I may have been responsible for the appointment of Attorney General John Ashcroft, who believes that what sets the United States apart from all other countries is that here "we have no king but Jesus." I grew up in Missouri, which has usually sent relatively sensible senators to Washington, and I'd found Senator Ashcroft, well, embarrassing. I didn't mind his speaking in tongues; it was the stuff he said in English that bothered me. When Ashcroft's opponent in the 2000 race was killed in a plane crash too late for his name to be removed from the ballot, I had a talk with the Almighty. I said that if He could see His way clear to having Ashcroft lose to someone who wasn't even alive, any other results of the election would be okay with me.

I had nothing to do, however, with the appointment of Condoleezza Rice, who told us that if Saddam wasn't removed the next smoking gun could be a mushroom cloud, or of Harvey Pitt, a lawyer for accounting firms who, as SEC chairman, somehow did not prove to be the perfect person to reform accounting firms. Nor am I to be blamed for the Sissy Hawk Brigade—that gaggle of neoconservatives, Vietnam draft evaders to a man, who finally found a president vulnerable to their cockamamie theories and thus brought us the war with Iraq. I had never even heard of Lieutenant General William Boykin, the Defense Department's Deputy Secretary for Intelligence (of all things), before he briefly made the papers by saying that Allah couldn't carry our God's glove. My responsibility for this mess is clearly defined and limited.

THE ONLY KING WE HAVE IS JESUS
(A Newly Unearthed Gospel Song Credited to John Ashcroft)

As I told the Bob Jones students,
Seated white and black apart,
This nation is unique, not like the rest.
As I faced those godly youngsters,
I told them from the heart
Just why this land will always be the best:

The only king we have is Jesus,
And I feel blessed to bring that news.
The only king we have is Jesus.
I can't explain why we've got Jews.

So because our king is Jesus,
I'm often heard to say,
Our kids should pray to Him each day in class.
If some kids just stay silent,
That's perfectly okay,
But they'll all be given Jesus tests to pass.

The only king we have is Jesus.
That's the truth we all perceive.
The only king we have is Jesus,
So Hindus may just have to leave.

Now Jesus hates abortion,
'Cause Jesus loves all life.
They call it choice; it's murder all the same.
The killers must be punished—
The doctor, man, and wife.
We'll execute them all in Jesus' name.

The only king we have is Jesus.
It's Jesus who can keep us pure.
The only king we have is Jesus,
And He's Republican for sure.

The homosexual lifestyle
Could make our Jesus weep.
He loathed their jokes about which cheek to turn.
Yes, Jesus came to teach us
With whom we're supposed to sleep.
Ignore that and you'll go to hell to burn.

(FINAL CHORUS SUNG IN TONGUES)
Tron smleck gha dreednus hoke b'loofnok
Frak fag narst fag madoondah greeb.
Tron smleck gha dreednus hoke b'loofnok
Dar popish, flarge dyur darky, hebe.

—FEBRUARY 5, 2001

33

NEW FEDERAL HiRES

So Elliott Abrams (the felon) is back,
And Poindexter's now a big cheese.
High-level appointments now favor the guys
With rap sheets instead of CVs.

—DECEMBER 30, 2002

REPUBLiCAN ANGER AT TRENT LOTT

Republicans feel anger, unconcealed,
Because Trent Lott revealed what he revealed.
They've always reassured the racist clods
By using code, festooned with winks and nods.
But now Lott's blown the gaff, for, once he'd spoken,
The world could see the Southern race-code broken.

—JANUARY 6, 2003

ON THE REVELATION OF WILLIAM BENNETT'S GAMBLING HABIT

Bill Bennett told a grateful nation,
"Be moral. Just resist temptation."
By windbag airing of this thesis,
Bill Bennett got as rich as Croesus.
His preaching sold in wholesale lots,
While he dropped millions at the slots.
But here's a thought to ease his pains:
He only lost ill-gotten gains.

—MAY 26, 2003

DISSENT

Now Ashcroft says his critics aid
An enemy whose plans are laid
To turn our torch of liberty quite dim.
So we should say, "Do what you please,
Forget the usual guarantees"—
Unless, of course, the enemy is
Him.

—JANUARY 7, 2002

JUST SPECULATiNG

Loose sixties morals, Gingrich said,
Was where our troubles lay.
Then Newt himself was found to have
A tendency to stray.

Rush Limbaugh has been hooked on pills,
While Bennett's hooked on slots.
Do all the right-wing morals police
Have copybooks with blots?

Does Falwell have a floozie, say,
Does Ashcroft, you suppose,
Get home from church and swiftly snort
Some white stuff up his nose?

Does Robertson crave demon rum?
Does Cheney make clerks promise
To hide the fact he's renting tapes
Last viewed by Clarence Thomas?

—NOVEMBER 3, 2003

ON GENERAL BOYKIN'S COMMENTS THAT HiS GOD'S BiGGER THAN THE iSLAM GOD ("NYA-NYA, NA, NYA-NYA")

The general says Islam's god's so small
He's just an idol, not a god at all.
The man's a moderate. Yes, you can cite
Much worse from zealots of the Christian right
(The gang that made a lapdog of Bush One,
And won the nomination for his son).
From Graham, Falwell, Robertson, and such
You hear that Islam's wicked, inasmuch
As evil was the Prophet's stock in trade.
A worthy target of a great crusade,
He was, they say, a killer and a thief
Whose terroristic forces caused much grief.
It's not just that Muhammad's god is teeny,
Muhammad's made to sound like Mussolini.
From Bush, this sort of language from these kooks
Produces just the mildest of rebukes.
He knows from Reverend Rove he has to keep
These shepherds happy, since he needs their sheep.
Another Bushie pooch lies still—perhaps
A different dog, but in the same old laps.

—NOVEMBER 24, 2003

ON TWO MEMBERS OF THE WAR CABINET

DON RUMSFELD MEETS THE PRESS

With condescending smile so tight,
He seems to take a great delight
Explaining to the press this fight,
As if they're kids who aren't too bright.
When wrong he needn't be contrite:
Don't might and arrogance make right?

COLIN POWELL, ALAS

His memory of war was strong.
No Sissy Hawk, he'd fought the Cong.
He knew that bunk on nukes was wrong.
But, still, he chose to go along.
Of him, they'll sing the saddest song:
"But, still, he chose to go along."

—NOVEMBER 17, 2003

WHAT TOM DELAY MIGHT HAVE HAD IN MIND WHEN HE HATCHED THE SHORT-LIVED SCHEME TO USE A CRUISE SHIP IN NEW YORK HARBOR DURING THE REPUBLICAN NATIONAL CONVENTION

"A cruise ship in the harbor," thought DeLay,
"Could be a place where decent folks would stay,
Avoiding all that mob that we detest—
New Yorkers, who are foreigners at best.
We'd still get pictures showing Bush as hero
While speaking resolutely at Ground Zero.
A pity it's to Sodom we must drag
Our George to get him wrapped up in the flag."

—DECEMBER 29, 2003

REACTION IN THE JUSTICE DEPARTMENT TO FEDERAL APPEALS COURTS RULING "WAR ON TERRORISM" DETENTION POLICIES UNCONSTITUTIONAL

A right to counsel and a right to trial?
John Ashcroft wonders: How do you suppose
We'll save our freedoms and our way of life
If we start granting everybody those?

—JANUARY 12, 2004

ON ANTONIN SCALIA'S EXPLANATION OF WHY DUCK HUNTING WITH DICK CHENEY AS CHENEY'S CASE COMES BEFORE THE COURT IS PERFECTLY OKAY

This criticism Nino calls absurd.
It's true that Quackscam is an ugly word.

He says that simple folks—the likes of us—
Show ignorance by making such a fuss
About some guys who often fly deluxe
In White House planes to blinds for shooting ducks.
Unless, of course, we've hung with shahs or rockers,
We just can't grasp the lives of big *k'nockers.*
There are, he plainly told the ones who'd jeered,
Some people too important to be *shmeered.*

The strongest point he made was when he wrote
That such a trip could hardly change his vote.
That's one thing that his critics can't rebut:
He'd vote for Cheney's side no matter what,
Then find some case law more or less in line.
If others do the same, that's five of nine.
You think they haven't done such things before?
Get law books out, and look up Bush v. Gore.

—APRIL 12, 2004

Part 5

BiG SHOTS ON CRiME SPREE;
BiLLiONS LOOTED;
FEW ARRESTS MADE

GEORGE W. BUSH AND DICK CHENEY LECTURE
CEOS ON CORPORATE RESPONSIBILITY

"Creative accounting" is something we hate.

From now on your numbers will have to be straight.

No taking of options for stock you contrive

To dump when insiders can tell it will dive.

And loans? If you want one, then go to the bank.

These sweetheart loans stink! They're disgusting! They're
   rank!

This type of behavior we strictly forbid.

Just do as we say now, and not as we did.

—AUGUST 19, 2002

The corporate scandals early in the Bush Administration—the collapse of the Enron shell game, the revelations of stock manipulations and accounting frauds, the spectacle of overpaid CEOs clinging to their private planes and corporate boxes like little boys trying to hoard all the Legos in the day-care center—involved a number of people close to the White House. Enron's CEO, Kenneth Lay, who had been intertwined with the Bush family for at least twenty years, even had one of those prized nicknames handed out by George W. Bush—although at least it wasn't something like Books Cooker.

Bush distanced himself from the malefactors. At one point he even said that Lay "was a supporter of Ann Richards in my run in 1994." Lay and other Enron executives had indeed contributed to Richards's campaign, but had given several times more money to the Bush campaign. (I once suggested that the corporate practice of donating to both candidates in an election could serve as a one-question admissions examination for political science graduate school: Explain this custom in a short essay without using the word "bribe.")

In fact, both the President and the Vice President had themselves been associated with precisely the sort of finagling that was being revealed, Cheney as the CEO of Halliburton while some dicey accounting practices were going on and Bush as a director of Harken Energy who managed to dump his Harken stock just before it collapsed. When Bush spoke soberly on how confidence in the free market required corporate honesty and transparency, he sounded a bit like Claude Rains expressing shock while closing down Rick's Bar for gambling.

A SPIRITED DEFENSE OF GEORGE W. BUSH AGAINST ACCUSATIONS THAT HE DUMPED HIS HARKEN STOCK BECAUSE OF INSIDE INFORMATION

He says he had no clue the stock would tank.
About the details he is still evasive.
Though "on the board but ignorant" seems lame,
With Bush, a clueless claim can sound persuasive.

—AUGUST 5, 2002

THE SINKING OF THE U.S.S. ENRON—A FREE MARKET METAPHOR

The pirate ship has sunk beneath the waves.
The swabs who haven't gone to wat'ry graves
Row desperately, though all of them now know
Their water and their food are running low.
They row their wretched boats, and curse their lot.
Receding in the distance is a yacht
That carries all their officers, who knew
The ship was doomed, but didn't tell the crew.
The officers stand tall. They saw their duty:
Desert the ship by night, and take the booty.

—FEBRUARY 4, 2002

OH, KENNY BOY
(A Houston Version of the Irish Folk Song)

Oh, Kenny Boy, your friends are disappearing.
They don't know you, much less your kvetchy wife.
Yes, it's so sad when pols that you've been schmeering
Now hope that you'll get twenty years to life.
They sang your song: they pushed deregulation.
They passed your laws. They bent the regs your way.
But now they track your every obfuscation.
Old Kenny Boy, their Kenny Boy's now Mister Lay.

—MARCH 4, 2002

THE BALLAD OF HARVEY PiTT

(With apologies to Stephen Sondheim and his demon barber)

Attend the tale of Harvey Pitt,
Who many thought was quite unfit
To choose who'll be the referees
For people who'd paid him those fabulous fees.
It didn't seem a perfect fit
For Harvey Pitt,
The fox who guarded the henhouse.

John Biggs was set to head the board,
But big accounting firms abhorred
The thought of someone so severe.
So little birds whispered in Harvey Pitt's ear:
"Hi, Harvey.
Yes. Harvey Pitt,
Our fox who's guarding the henhouse:

Rid yourself of Biggs, Harvey. Biggs might know too much.
What we need's a guy who's just a bit out of touch."

But who instead would Pitt recruit?
He'd need a man of high repute,
A man whose reputation's grand—
Accomplished, but not in the matter at hand.

"Judge Webster's it,"
Said Harvey Pitt,
The fox who guarded the henhouse.

The judge was hardly a CPA.
Pitt, though, managed to win the day.
He had the votes. He didn't tell:
Webster's boards also emitted a smell.
Harvey'd shot himself in the foot.
This meant Harvey was done—kaput.
Saying the truth wouldn't have been brainy:
"Webster is cleaner than Bush or than Cheney."
Harvey, Harvey, Harvey, Harvey, Harvey

Attend the tale of Harvey Pitt,
Who thought he needn't be legit
To regulate the SEC
For people as fond of the foxes as he.
Bye, Harvey,
Poor Harvey Pitt,
The fox who guarded the henhouse.

—NOVEMBER 25, 2002

Part 6

LOBBYISTS, HEIRESSES, AND OTHERS IN NEED OF COMPASSION

A REPUBLICAN DISCUSSES TAXES

Because they pay too much in taxes—
To feed the poor and fight the axis—
The rich are truly discommoded.
It spoils the fun of being loaded.
So we should tax the poor instead—
A tax on alms, or day-old bread.

—FEBRUARY 3, 2003

*W*hatever the Republican Party's policy on taxes happens to be called—supply-side economics or stimulation of the economy or avoiding double taxation—it has always rested on the same simple, unvarying proposition: If rich people paid less in taxes, we'd all be better off.

George W. Bush would hardly be the person to question this proposition—he suffers from what Robert MacNeil has called "a dangerous incuriosity"—and his Administration also followed an undeviating corporate line on such issues as energy and the environment. Its energy policies, put together by a task force of people the White House refused to name, were eventually reflected in an energy bill described by John McCain as "leave no lobbyist behind." In a speech dismissing energy conservation as little more than a feel-good sop, Dick Cheney spoke with the same condescension he would later employ when discussing the futility of depending on United Nations inspectors in Iraq to find the nuclear arms that everyone knew Saddam Hussein had.

Environmental regulations that industry found uncomfortable were relaxed—not surprisingly, since the people chosen for regulatory posts tended to be people who had previously made a living as lobbyists trying to get environmental regulations relaxed. When the regulation in question governed the level of arsenic in drinking water, I remembered what was said years ago by an industry spokesman in Texas during a controversy over pollution in the Houston Ship Channel: "Arsenic is a scare word."

ON THE GRADUAL END OF THE ESTATE TAX

For years, estates of wealthy men were taxed—
The sort of thing that spoils a nice good-bye.
The tax will fade away in nine more years.
And then the rich will find it safe to die.

—JUNE 18, 2001

THE REPUBLICAN PLAN TO STIMULATE THE ECONOMY

It's very hard to estimate
Just what it takes to stimulate
A corporation, but we know
These people need a lot of dough,
And so, if no one else objects,
We'll cut them some humongous checks.
But stimulating them is tough.
A billion may not be enough
To spur a corporation while
It keeps its CEO in style.
It's possible we should explore
Some way that we can give them more.
We may just give them all we've got:
It takes a lot to get them hot.

—DECEMBER 3, 2001

A RiSE iN UNEMPLOYMENT ARRiVES ON SCHEDULE

You cannot find a job? No cash is flowing?
You haven't paid your bills, which have been growing?
You'll never get the money you've been owing?
Be happy: The economy is slowing.

The strategy is working fine.
It's not a time for you to whine.

You're running out of things that you can sell?
Your health insurance just ran out as well?
Your life is an unmitigated hell?
Be happy, for the Dow's responding well.

So try to take the macro view.
It's not about just little you.

—JUNE 26, 2000

ON BUSH BREAKING HIS CAMPAIGN PLEDGE
TO LIMIT CARBON-DIOXIDE EMISSIONS

Yes, W once took the view
That CO_2 is bad for you.
He says he's had a turnabout:
We make this stuff when breathing out,
So dangerous is what it's not.
From lobbyists you learn a lot.

—APRIL 9, 2001

ON THE BUSH ADMINISTRATION RESCINDING LIMITS
OF ARSENIC IN DRINKING WATER

Though arsenic's in what we drink,
It's not as nasty as you think.
Yes, hidden in the stroganoff
It's used for knocking people off.
But in your water it's okay—
That's what the mining interests say.
Apparently, in Bush's view
It mixes well with CO_2.

—APRIL 16, 2001

DEPARTMENT OF EARTH SECURITY

The EPA cites chapter, and some verse,
To show this warming's making matters worse.
It's getting worse no matter how you score it.
So here's the plan: They think we should ignore it.

—JULY 1, 2002

GEORGE W. BUSH'S EDUCATION PLAN

A public school whose students don't test well
Would lose its funds unless its score improves.
If cutting funds won't help the kids advance,
We could prohibit lunch, or take their shoes.

—OCTOBER 4, 1999

ON THE BUSH ADMINISTRATION'S REVERSAL OF ITS ANNOUNCEMENT THAT TESTING SCHOOL LUNCH MEAT FOR SALMONELLA WOULD NO LONGER BE REQUIRED

They'll check for salmonella, kids.
It's safe as mozzarella, kids.
Light up a panatela, kids.
You've nothing more to fear.

Give thanks for this new fella, kids.
Sing praises a cappella, kids.
Let Bush be your umbrella, kids.
Compassion's finally here.

—APRIL 30, 2001

GEORGE W. BUSH SPEAKS OUT ON GAY MARRIAGE

He backs an amendment defining the vow
Of marriage as being a guy and his *frau*
Lest civilization sink into a slough—
Which he says could happen. It isn't clear how.

Though he can't explain it, he needn't expand.
We saw this with Poppy. We know what's at hand:
The Jesus battalions demanded this stand.
The yelp of the lapdog is heard in the land.

REPRISE:
He is a onetime lapdog's son, so it may not strike anyone
As odd that he's content to run as one who's to the left of
    none—a Robertson Republican.

—MARCH 22, 2004

Part 7

JUST iNVADE SOMETHiNG

WE SPEAK NOT OF OSAMA

(With apologies to Cole Porter, the master,
who wrote "My Heart Belongs to Daddy")

The towers fell. We knew full well
The villain in this awful drama.
His name held sway, 'til he got away,
Now we speak not of Osama.

We said we'd pound him once he's found
So flat that he'd cry for his momma.
Forget that jive, that "dead or alive,"
'Cause we speak not of Osama.

He's not even in the axis.
No, his evil did not make the grade.
For the thing he mostly lacks is
A country that we can invade.

He could be in Yokohama,
Or Bahrain or Belize or Dubai.
But to get back at Osama
We'll just pulverize some other guy.

—MARCH 3, 2003

*L*ike a birthday party organized around a theme, America's view of the world often seems to be organized around a Demon in Chief. For years, the Demon in Chief was Fidel Castro. Muammar al-Qaddafi was the Demon in Chief for a while. A foreign affairs graduate student could probably chart the staying power of Demons in Chief by attending the Greenwich Village Halloween parade every year and counting the villain masks.

Osama bin Laden must have had the shortest run as Demon in Chief since Manuel Noriega. After the attacks of September 11, George W. Bush, declaring a war on terrorism, said we would go to Afghanistan or anywhere else to bring bin Laden back, "dead or alive." The Taliban, who had been harboring bin Laden, were defeated. As usual, the country rallied behind a wartime president. George W. Bush saw his approval ratings soar.

But bin Laden couldn't be found. The White House had a bold response: It quit uttering his name. Absent a Demon in Chief, though, the war on terrorism seemed a bit hollow. Eventually, despite a new Homeland Security Department and color-coded alerts and exquisitely ornate security precautions at airports, the country seemed to settle back into peacetime, always a more problematic time for whoever occupies the White House.

It now appears that Saddam Hussein sent word through back channels that he would meet all American demands in order to avoid an invasion, but there was one factor he may have failed to appreciate about the United States: You can't be a wartime president without a war.

ON THE APPOINTMENT OF HENRY KISSINGER, THAT CHAMPION OF OPENNESS IN GOVERNMENT, TO CHAIR THE 9/11 INQUIRY

> "Mr. Kissinger said today that he was not aware that any of his
> clients might pose conflicts of interest with his mission as chairman
> of the commission, which is to investigate why the United States
> failed to prevent the attacks." —*THE NEW YORK TIMES*

There are no conflicts to prevent
This mystery from being solved.
From that we can at least conclude
That Pinochet was not involved.

—DECEMBER 23, 2002

RUDY GIULIANI, WHO SAW NEW YORK THROUGH 9/11, IS HONORED BY TIME MAGAZINE

So Rudy is the person of the year.
We join the world in offering a cheer.
At certain times, it now must be conceded,
A paranoid control freak's just what's needed.

—JANUARY 21, 2002

RUNNING OUT OF TARGETS IN AFGHANISTAN
(A Pilot's Lament)

We're running out of targets, guys,
There's nothing to destroy.
They simply don't have buildings here,
Like Baghdad or Hanoi.

Today I sent a missile off
And said, "That's all she wrote."
It turned out that I'd vaporized
Two camels and a goat.

So let's go back to Serbia.
These gunsights have to glom
On something that's not rocks or sand.
There's nothing here to bomb.

—NOVEMBER 19, 2001

A TWO-PRONGED APPROACH TO THE AFGHAN PEOPLE

By night our missiles rain on them,
By day we drop them bread.
They should be grateful for the food—
Unless, of course, they're dead.

—OCTOBER 29, 2001

SLEEP TiGHT
(A Lullaby Sung Each Night to Osama bin Laden)

Sleep tight. There's no one making much ado.
So sleep this night, Big O—in peace, sleep through it.
The folks you bombed now never mention you.
They're chasing down a guy who didn't do it.

—SEPTEMBER 1, 2003

EVERYTHiNG GEORGE BUSH NEEDS TO KNOW
HE LEARNED ON THE PLAYGROUND

Let's say that from the east while you look south
An icy snowball hits you in the mouth.
You see the kid who did it run, the wretch,
But he proves quite impossible to catch.
He's gone. So you, your anger quite unsated,
Beat up another kid you've always hated.

You hit him from above and underneath.
Then smash his nose and rearrange his teeth.
Yes, pound on him until that dreadful punk'll
Have no alternative to crying uncle.
Though he is not the wretch too fast to chase,
It's hard to tell that once you've smashed his face.

—APRIL 28, 2003

ON PAUL O'NEILL'S REVELATION THAT THE BUSHMEN WERE PLANNING A WAR WITH IRAQ FROM THE EARLIEST DAYS OF THE ADMINISTRATION

It now appears that they saw 9/11
As, even though not quite ordained in heaven
To punish godless sins allowed in bed
(As Falwell and Pat Robertson had said),
At least a blow that could be put to use—
Though tragic, sure, a heaven-sent excuse.

—FEBRUARY 9, 2004

THE 9/11 COMMISSION HEARS FROM RICHARD CLARKE

When testimony came from Richard Clarke, he
Inspired White House spokesmen to get snarky,
Because, with words combining bite and bark, he
Revealed their tough-guy pose as pure malarkey.

—APRIL 19, 2004

Part 8

ASSORTED IRRELEVANT COUNTRIES

BUiLDiNG A COALiTiON, W-STYLE

We'll talk to Germany and France,
Brief Russians and Chinese,
Consult with Turkey and Japan,
Then do just as we please.

—SEPTEMBER 30, 2002

he first President Bush painstakingly put together an international coalition to eject Saddam Hussein's troops from Kuwait. That wasn't George W. Bush's style. If the United Nations did not believe that the time for war with Iraq had come—even though Saddam Hussein's defiance of UN resolutions was at times the reason the Administration gave for the necessity of military action—the United Nations was making itself irrelevant. If France didn't agree with our line of reasoning, it was perfidious or showing itself to be part of Old Europe. In March of 2003, Administration supporters in Congress said that French fries would henceforth be listed on the menu of congressional cafeterias as freedom fries. This did not bring the French to heel.

Although we were constantly assured that even Old Europe would join our coalition against Iraq once the crunch came, the architects of the war actually seemed to prefer going it alone. In their reasoning, that was the way the United States would shake off the Vietnam malaise and make the rest of the world quake before the might of the last remaining superpower. Eventually, of course, military resistance in a country that we had supposedly already conquered was enough to force the last remaining superpower to schedule a hasty turnover of political authority, lest the disaster show itself most vividly during the American presidential election campaign. Among the other nations of the world, there was no discernible quaking.

ON THE BACKLASH AGAINST THE PERFIDIOUS FRENCH

They're relegated to the side.
This role—which they cannot abide,
Which torments Frenchmen day and night—
Can make them do things out of spite.
But could it be the French are right?

And, yes, it sometimes makes one boil
To see what they will do for oil.
For when it comes to heat and light,
Their principles are not in sight.
But could it be the French are right?

And, sure, they come on rather strong
If you pronounce a diphthong wrong.
And even if you're quite contrite,
They often fail to be polite.
But could it be the French are right?

Yes, could it be these French, despite
The things about them you could cite
(That what they write is often quite
Confused as well as recondite,
That all this Gallic appetite
For food and wine can seem so trite,
That they don't love to stand and fight,
Nor bathe as often as they might),
By chance are in this instance right?

—MARCH 10, 2003

THE SAUDIS AND THEIR OIL RIGS

(Sung to the tune of "The Farmer and the Cowman" from Oklahoma*)*

The Saudis and their oil rigs are our friends.
Oh, the Saudis and their oil rigs are our friends.
They can bomb us when they please, we need gas for SUVs.
We're infidels, but we can make amends.
Petrobusiness pals must stick together.
All the guzzlers' gas tanks must be filled.
We'll protect the Saudis' border
While they preach we should be killed.
They teach their kids the Protocols of Zion.
It's jail for women if their hair is showing.
They say that we're corrupt and that we're wicked.
We say, "Whatever. Keep that petrol flowing."
Petrobusiness pals must stick together.
All the guzzlers' gas tanks must be filled.
We'll protect the Saudis' border
While they preach we should be killed.

—MAY 20, 2002

AN ANALYSIS OF THE TURKISH-AMERICAN ALLIANCE, ITS DIPLOMATIC SIGNIFICANCE, AND ITS ROLE IN ESTABLISHING DEMOCRACY IN THE MIDDLE EAST

Get allies? That's not hard to do.
We'll simply go and buy a few.

—MARCH 17, 2003

THE KURDS ARE IN THE WAY AGAIN

The Kurds are in the way again,
And so, to our dismay again,
If we begin a fray again,
As it appears we may again,
It seems we must betray again
The Kurds: They're in the way again.

—MARCH 24, 2003

A NEW, SiMPLER ANALYSiS OF THE RECENT BUSH-PUTiN SUMMiT

Bush and Putin talk together,
To each other's charms succumb.
Bush thinks Putin can be trusted.
Putin thinks that Bush is dumb.

Bush and Putin end their meeting,
Smile until their mouths are numb.
Bush thinks Putin can be trusted.
Putin thinks that Bush is dumb.

Now that they have met each other,
Each has got a rule of thumb:
Bush thinks Putin can be trusted.
Putin thinks that Bush is dumb.

—JULY 16, 2001

ON KiM JONG iL'S ANNOUNCEMENT

We said that Kim Jong Il was just the guy
For whom we needed Star Wars in the sky.
Now Kim Jong Il declares we needn't worry
That he might up and bomb us in a hurry:
He isn't testing for the missile race;
He's got a moratorium in place.
Does this, then, mean that we won't have to wield
A multi-billion-dollar missile shield?
Well, no, for other wicked rogues remain.
If they go, we'll find others as profane.
If all rogues disappear, we won't be glum,
We'll hope that if we build it they will come.

—AUGUST 20, 2001

THOUGHTS ON GEOPOLITICS

It seemed like such a good idea.
Oh, when did it begin to sour,
And start to be no fun to be
The last remaining superpower?

—OCTOBER 20, 2003

Part 9

THE CHARGE OF THE
SiSSY HAWK BRiGADE

RICHARD PERLE: WHOSE FAULT IS HE?

Consider kids who bullied Richard Perle—
Those kids who said Perle threw just like a girl,
Those kids who poked poor Perle to show how soft
A momma's boy could be, those kids who oft
Times pushed poor Richard down and could be heard
Addressing him as Sissy, Wimp, or Nerd.
Those kids have got a lot to answer for,
'Cause Richard Perle now wants to start a war.
The message his demeanor gets across:
He'll show those playground bullies who's the boss.
He still looks soft, but when he writes or talks
There is no tougher dude among the hawks.
And he's got planes and ships and tanks and guns—
All manned, of course, by other people's sons.

—SEPTEMBER 16, 2002

*I*n an uncharacteristically prankish mood, I wrote that poem without knowing anything about Richard Perle's childhood. After it appeared, though, I heard from one of Perle's grade school classmates, who wanted to know how I'd found out that Perle had been bullied. Then another classmate wrote *The Nation,* saying that she didn't remember Perle as a wimp but as simply "very serious." After gathering some true details, I answered Perle's defender in *The Nation:* "You were not one of the fourth-grade girls who used to push Richard down the hill on Fuller Street, and you didn't laugh once in sixth grade when Rocco Guntermann, from Mrs. Flynn's class, referred to Richard as 'Perlie Girl'? Fine. Whatever you say. If the United States invades Iraq without provocation, it won't be your fault."

She wrote again. She remembered Fuller Street and Mrs. Flynn, but she claimed there was no Rocco Guntermann. My final answer in the letters column was, "I suppose Rocco Guntermann, the classmate whose existence you deny, did not say to me just last week, 'We can settle this if Perlie Girl meets me near the swings at five o'clock on Friday, and tell him not to bring two teachers and his mother this time.' Would it surprise you to learn that Rocco is now a psychotherapist in Sherman Oaks?"

Another letter asked why I didn't use the word *chicken hawk* to describe Perle and his flock. A chicken hawk, which exists in nature, is a hawk that preys on chickens, not a hawk that acts like a chicken. A sissy hawk acts like a sissy.

ON RICHARD PERLE—LOBBYIST, BUSINESSMAN, AND, PERHAPS NOT COINCIDENTALLY, CHAIRMAN OF THE DEFENSE POLICY BOARD

The plans to start this war were laid
Within the Sissy Hawk Brigade—
A band of Vietnam evaders
All puffed up now as tough crusaders.
Yes, now, as then, they love inciting
A war that others will be fighting.

In recent weeks, there's been much talk
Of Richard Perle, a sissy hawk.
There've been some articles about
Just whether Perle has used his clout,
While fighting evil hell-for-leather,
To profit. (Hawks have nests to feather.)

A pity that some lads who fought
In Vietnam were later brought
Back home again in body bags
Adorned with battle stars and flags:
They missed the fruits that dedication
Can bring to those who serve their nation.

—APRIL 14, 2003

ON THE RESIGNATION OF RICHARD PERLE, CAPTAIN OF THE SISSY HAWK BRIGADE, FROM THE CHAIRMANSHIP OF THE DEFENSE POLICY BOARD

And so for Richard Perle was writ
The second graf of his obit:
This soaring bird of hawkish myth
Was grounded when discovered with
His talon in the cookie jar
While reaching for a small *pourboire.*[*]

    [*]To use Old Europe's language, French,
    May seem to hawks contrarian.
    Pardon. Our friends have changed too fast
    For me to learn Bulgarian.

—APRIL 21, 2003

A SISSY HAWK CHEER

Bomb 'em now, kill 'em now, zim, boom, bah
Sissy hawks, sissy hawks, rah, rah, rah.
Vietnam reverberates.
(We were rooting from the States.)
All-out war is still our druthers—
Fiercely fought, and fought by others.
Hit 'em now, before things worsen.
We love war, though not in person.
Bomb 'em now, kill 'em now, zim, boom, bah
Sissy hawks, sissy hawks, rah, rah, rah.

—OCTOBER 28, 2002

PAUL WOLFOWITZ AS A GUEST AT THE AL RASHEED HOTEL WHEN IT IS ATTACKED BY ROCKETS

He's been this war's great glorifier.
With Vietnam, he seemed much shier:
He didn't think that war'd require
Himself. No grunt, his goals were higher.
The situation's getting dire:
A Sissy Hawk's been under fire.

—NOVEMBER 17, 2003

A SHORT CONVERSATiON WiTH A SiSSY HAWK ON THE POSSiBiLiTY OF A QUAGMiRE

"The nerve! Not so! That word still rankles."
"You're sinking. I can't see your ankles."
"The thugs are here; we now just squeeze."
"Excuse me: It's above your knees."
"We planned all this; it's no surprise."
"There's nothing showing 'neath your thighs."
"With terrorists brute force works best."
"I think the mud's now at your chest."
"To show our strength, we have to drub
These . . . Arab . . . glub, glub, glub, glub, glub."

—SEPTEMBER 22, 2003

Part 10

THE CROOKED PATH
TO WAR

A SCHOLARLY ANALYSIS OF DEVELOPMENTS
(INCLUDING SATELLITE PHOTOS, INTELLIGENCE REPORTS, AND
MIDDLE-EASTERN STRATEGY CONSIDERATIONS) THAT PERSUADED
THE BUSH ADMINISTRATION THAT ITS POLICY ON DEALING WITH
IRAQ HAD TO CHANGE FROM ECONOMIC SANCTIONS TO
PREEMPTIVE WAR

Osama's split and Wall Street's sagging.
It's time to get that puppy wagging.

—OCTOBER 7, 2002

*a*m I saying that the invasion of Iraq was a diversion, as in the movie *Wag the Dog*? I am saying, at least, that Iraq's threat to American society might have been seen by the White House as less imminent if the Dow had been at twelve thousand and Osama bin Laden had been in a cage in Guantanamo. I am saying that the desire to follow Afghanistan with a second act was among a number of elements that led George W. Bush to buy the Sissy Hawk Plan for World Domination that his father had wisely rejected. The second act, we were assured, would be even easier than the first, with the Sissy Hawks' proconsul-in-waiting—Ahmed Chalabi, the man from Armani—striding through a blizzard of flower petals to become the new ruler of Iraq.

Of course, the multiple reasons behind the decision to go to war were not the reasons offered to the public, which might have found them less impressive than warnings from George W. Bush and Dick Cheney and Condoleezza (Mushroom Cloud) Rice and Colin Powell that we had specific and definite knowledge of Iraq's weapons of mass destruction.

After months of Administration officials conflating 9/11 and Iraq at any opportunity—at one point, seventy percent of Americans believed Saddam had been responsible—Bush finally acknowledged, long after the invasion, that there was no evidence of Iraqi involvement. It was a casual statement, as if he'd said that, contrary to a previous announcement, he'd be spending the weekend at Camp David rather than at the ranch.

WAR AGAINST IRAQ: THE CONTEXT

The terrorism war begins to sag.
The perpetrator we were meant to bag
Remains at large, and wartime fervor fades.
Then Bush and all his hawkish White House aides
Drop sanctions as the way to tame Iraq
And say, "Without delay, we must attack."
If that war sags, there's still a backup plan.
It's war without delay against Iran.
And when the zest for that war, too, has faded?
That's easy: North Korea gets invaded.
But then it's hard to think of what to do.
Destroy Bahrain? Bomb France? Invade Peru?

—SEPTEMBER 23, 2002

THE SILVER LINING OF SUPREME COMMANDER ROVE'S VICTORY IN THE MIDTERM ELECTIONS

The talk of war has done its job.
Rove's hopes were far exceeded.
So maybe, with the voting done,
The war itself's not needed.

—DECEMBER 2, 2002

WARS

(A preventive-war anthem sung to the tune that Joyce Kilmer's
"Trees" was set to, with piano accompaniment)

We think that God has never made
A country we should not invade.
Some evil tyrants go unchecked,
And bombing them gets us respect.
The more small countries we destroy
The more respect we can enjoy.

La-da-dee-dee, bomb-bomb.
La-da-dee-dee, bomb-bomb.

And rulers who may seem okay?
It's smart to bomb them anyway,
So others fear us like the Hun.
That Vietnam disease is done.
Our country had it wrong before:
There's nothing better than a war.

—MAY 12, 2003

TWO BAD GUYS

This Kim Jong Il's a naughty lad,
But Bush says he's not half as bad
As ol' Saddam, whom we must swat
Before he gets what Kim has got.
Though both are in the evil axis,
Saddam gets hit, while Kim relaxes,
And why? What do our leaders say?
The reason changes every day.

—FEBRUARY 10, 2003

THERE'S NO! NO! IN YOUR EYES
(As Sung to Saddam Hussein by George W. Bush)

(With apologies to Eddy Howard, and anybody
who becomes collateral damage)

Saddam, we've threatened to attack
If you keep weapons masked.
Don't think you'll now avoid a war
By doing what we've asked.

Your lips tell me yes, yes,
But there's no, no in your eyes.
So stop saying you're okaying
Our inspections. Realize,
Lacking backing, we're attacking,
Whatever your replies.
Your lips tell me yes, yes,
But there's no, no in your eyes.

—OCTOBER 14, 2002

INSPECTIONS: THE WHITE HOUSE FALLBACK POSITION

If nothing shows in spy-plane pics
And Blix finds nothing in the sticks,
That still won't put us in a fix.
We'll blame it on Iraqi tricks,
And say, "So, Blix, just hit the bricks.
It's time that we got in our licks."

—DECEMBER 16, 2002

THE LOYAL OPPOSITION

The Senate Democrats sat mum,
Like doves afraid to coo.
So history will soon record
This war as their war too.

—APRIL 7, 2003

BUSH, CHENEY, RUMSFELD, AND, ALAS, POWELL TALK TO THE AMERICAN PEOPLE

They pushed the CIA to say
That nukes could quickly come our way—
Saddam might, with a finger snap,
Remove Chicago from the map.
They took a lack of proof in stride.
They simply lied.

Intelligence? The Pentagon's
Came straight from dorkish neocons
Employed to find Iraq in back
Of every terrorist attack.
When plain facts failed to serve their side,
They simply lied.

The war's opponents they'd deride
As wimps who'd like to run and hide
From threats we simply can't abide.
The Gulf of Tonkin was their guide:
They simply lied, and lied, and lied.

—JUNE 30, 2003

REACTiON TO THE PRESiDENT'S "MiSSiON ACCOMPLiSHED" APPEARANCE ON THE U.S.S. <u>ABRAHAM LiNCOLN</u> BY THOSE WHO SERVED iN GEORGE W. BUSH'S AiR NATiONAL GUARD UNiT BUT CAN'T SEEM TO REMEMBER SEEiNG HiM AROUND

When he lands on the deck in his flight suit
To impress all the sailors he's greeting,
It looks grand, but there's one thing we're thinking:
Does this count, then, as making a meeting?

—JUNE 9, 2003

ONE WAY GEORGE BUSH'S SURPRISE THANKSGIVING VISIT TO BAGHDAD (SORT OF) MAKES SENSE

Supreme Commander Rove, despite his power,
Watched, helpless, as his finest stunt went sour.
Off San Diego, he'd arranged, with glee,
A perfect picture, Victory at Sea:
The flight suit and the banner all just right,
The ship turned so the city's out of sight.
Air Guardsman Bush, responding to those greetings,
Made one forget he'd missed a year of meetings.
A poster shot! The candidate's in clover—
Or would have been had Bush's war been over.
If he can't staunch the stream of GI dead,
The Democrats may use that shot instead.
Supreme Commander Rove knew he must seek a
Replacement shot. And then he cried, "Eureka!"

—DECEMBER 22, 2003

NEW (SORT OF) ISSUE

Bush trotted out his whoppers with tranquility,
Because the press responded with docility.
His goal was war. In order to fulfill it, he
Exaggerated threats and volatility.
But now his tales are showing their fragility.
At last, the question's Bush's credibility.

Yes, suddenly, zap!
The man's got a gap.

—MARCH 8, 2004

A WORD TO GEORGE BUSH, ON THE OCCASION OF HIS MENTIONING THAT IRAQ WAS NOT RESPONSIBLE FOR THE ATTACKS ON 9/11

You tell us, with a casual by-the-way,
Iraq was not behind that awful day,
As if we'd never heard your staff and you
Implying just the opposite was true.
The Web must say, or maybe Lexis-Nexis,
If *chutzpa* is a word they use in Texas.

—OCTOBER 13, 2003

Part II

WHERE HAVE ALL THE
WEAPONS GONE?

WE'RE SAFE FROM SADDAM
(A Joyous Song of Deliverance for Spring)

We're safe from Saddam, tra-la, tra-la,
We're safe from Saddam, oh goody!
He can't send a bomb, tra-la, tra-la.
Which he could have done. Or could he?

—JUNE 16, 2003

*W*hen George W. Bush said that Iraq had been liberated from a brutal regime, he spoke for the nation—even for those churlish enough to point out that the regime's brutalities, all well-documented long before Bush took office, had previously not struck him or his top aides as the sort of thing our foreign policy should dwell on. But where were those weapons of mass destruction that made Iraq an imminent threat to our security?

Sometimes, discussion of them seemed to strike the President as tantamount to finding them. Sometimes, he spoke as if they hadn't been terribly important in the first place. It became obvious that his statement in the State of the Union speech about Iraq's purchase of uranium in Niger was known to be bunkum when he said it; a retired diplomat revealed that he had reported back as much after having been sent by the CIA to Niger to investigate. The Administration's response was to leak the fact that the former diplomat's wife was a CIA operative. No other administration had ever considered the identity of the lobbyists who had helped devise its energy policy a more important national secret than the identity of an undercover American intelligence agent.

I suggested a Zen question for Bush's next press conference: "Sir, if the ability of the Star Wars ABMs to hit a nuclear missile is imaginary and the nuclear missiles in Iraq are imaginary, does that mean a Star Wars ABM could hit an Iraqi nuclear missile? And, if so, would you consider that justification for having gone to war against Iraq?"

THE ADMINISTRATION'S ATTITUDE TOWARD THE SEARCH FOR WEAPONS OF MASS DESTRUCTION, WHOSE PRESENCE WAS THE REASON GIVEN (AT LEAST ON MONDAYS, THURSDAYS, AND ALTERNATE FRIDAYS) FOR WAGING PREVENTIVE WAR ON IRAQ

So maybe we will find them yet,
Well stashed away in some place clever.
Or were they just destroyed in March?
Or never there at all? Whatever.

—MAY 19, 2003

THE TRUTH EMERGES, SORT OF

Ah hah! So Tenet is the guy
Responsible for Bush's lie
About the Niger A-bomb deal
That from the start was quite unreal.
The Niger lie's off Tenet's chest.
So who's to blame for all the rest?

—AUGUST 4, 2003

JUST WAIT

The White House said, although it wasn't true,
Iraq must be invaded, PDQ,
Since terrorists, who'd caught us unaware,
Were with Iraq, and always gathered there.

They didn't then, but more come every day,
So they can drive the infidels away.
Will other lies come true? Can we deduce
That Baghdad's A-bomb plants will now produce?

—SEPTEMBER 15, 2003

SiXTEEN LiTTLE WORDS
(From the New Musical by George Bush and Karl Rove, <u>The Buck Stops There</u>)

First Tenet said, "The fault is mine.
I should have looked at every line."
Then someone at the NSC
Said, "No, George. Please. Not you. It's me."

It's everybody's fault except the boss's.
They're coming forth to take the blame in hordes.
They all say they're the one the albatross is.
There's clanging as they fall upon their swords.

Now Bush's aides are all contrite.
A queue is forming (on the right)—
All volunteers to claim that text.
A White House steward may be next.

It's everybody's fault except the boss's.
They're coming forth to take the blame in hordes.
They all say they're the one the albatross is.
There's clanging as they fall upon their swords.

The words that were the most persuasive
In turning citizens invasive
Had been exposed as bunk before.
But in a speech that pressed for war,
Those words described a looming threat.
So all the vetters failed to vet.

It's everybody's fault except the boss's.
They're coming forth to take the blame in hordes.
They all say they're the one the albatross is.
There's clanging as they fall upon their swords.

—AUGUST 18, 2003

THE PRESIDENT'S RESPONSE TO DAVID KAY'S INTERIM REPORT STATING THAT NO WEAPONS OF MASS DESTRUCTION HAVE BEEN FOUND IN IRAQ

The President now says that Kay's report—
Which plainly states that weapons of the sort
The White House said Iraq had all around
Cannot, despite a thorough search, be found—
Confirms that we were right to go to war
To smash those weapons flat forevermore.
You say that makes no sense? Well, you can grouse,
But then it's possible they'll smear your spouse.

—OCTOBER 27, 2003

SADDAM AS A GATHERING THREAT

So the weapons weren't there—so what, Bush says,
Saddam was a "gathering threat."
We were certainly right to start a war.
This threat simply had to be met.

A gathering threat can't be ignored,
So that's why we gave him a lathering.
Except if the weapons weren't there at all,
One wonders just what he was gathering.

—MARCH 1, 2004

ON WHETHER THE MARTHA STEWART GUILTY VERDICT CARRIES IMPLICATIONS FOR THOSE INVOLVED IN PREWAR INTELLIGENCE-GATHERING

When federal authorities come by,
It's criminal if you concoct a lie.
The feds don't think that lies are okey-dokey.
Will Chalabi, then, soon be in the pokey?
He plainly slipped the CIA some whoppers
Much larger than those Martha told the coppers.
Well, no, this liar won't be brought to book.
Although they knew their Ahmed was a crook,
His neoconnish sponsors wouldn't check
Those weapons legends that were plainly dreck.
One shrewd defense for him would work, it's clear:
"I only tell them what they want to hear."

—MARCH 29, 2004

EXPLAINING IN HIS STATE OF THE UNION ADDRESS WHY THE UNITED STATES INVADED AND OCCUPIED ANOTHER COUNTRY WITHOUT PROVOCATION, GEORGE W. BUSH OFFERS HISTORY HIS VERSION OF "REMEMBER PEARL HARBOR!"

Iraq had shown proclivities
For "weapons-of-mass-destruction-related program activities."

—FEBRUARY 23, 2004

Part 12

REPUBLICAN NATION BUILDING

"STATE DEPT. STUDY FORESAW TROUBLE iN iRAQ"
(Headline, The New York Times, October 19, 2003)

Before the war some working groups at State
Predicted problems certain to await
The occupying forces in Iraq.
But at Defense the neocons held sway.
They had contempt for viewpoints on the fray
That didn't come from them or from their claque.

They paid no mind to such defeatist talk.
They knew for sure the cakewalk that we'd walk
Would tame the Middle East with one great blow.
Iraq would pay its reconstruction bill.
Resistance, once we'd won, would soon be nil.
And what could striped-pants cookie-pushers know!

—NOVEMBER 10, 2003

*T*he sissy hawks had said that our troops would be greeted with flowers. Paul Wolfowitz testified to a congressional committee that Iraq could pay for its own reconstruction. Why would people that confident of success pay any attention to a report that laid out the difficulties ahead?

Trying to look on the bright side, I proposed a friendly question for that Bush press conference: "Sir, although the predictions of your supporters that Iraqis would greet our troops with flowers haven't been borne out, isn't it possible that, given the problems with the water supply and the infrastructure in general, there is a serious shortage of flowers over there and that Iraqis might be greeting our troops with flowers if Iraqis had any flowers?" The follow-up question was, "Mr. President, in your supplemental budget for the reconstruction of Iraq, is there any money specifically ear-marked for rebuilding the Iraqi cut-flower industry, and, if so, would any American company be able to bid on the contract or is Halliburton the only corporation with the resources and expertise to take on that job?"

Republican nation building! Spreading democracy had become the rallying cry for the very people who had dismissed as goody-goody any concern about human rights in foreign countries other than Cuba. The very president who had warned against America's becoming involved in nation building was talking about how many billions the infrastructure would cost. Fortunately, he had a few friends in the infrastructure business.

TO OLD EUROPE FROM THE LAST REMAINING SUPERPOWER: A POLITE REQUEST FOR HELP IN IRAQ

Well, yes, we may have used the word *appease*.
We may have called you weenies who munch cheese.
But now we're asking nicely for your aid—
To help clean up the awful mess we've made.
We'll run the show, of course. We always do:
We can't take orders from the likes of you.

—SEPTEMBER 29, 2003

ON THE HALLIBURTON CORPORATION'S NO-BID IRAQ CONTRACT

A lot of folks die.
At last the war ends.
The world is made safe
For Dick Cheney's friends.

—MAY 5, 2003

A SiLVER-LiNiNG ViEW OF GEORGE BUSH'S NOT ATTENDiNG MiLiTARY FUNERALS, LEST HE BECOME ASSOCiATED WiTH BAD NEWS

At least there's no Bush eulogy
On why they had to die.
It's better that they're laid to rest
Without another lie.

—DECEMBER 1, 2003

A PHOTO, WiTH CAPTiON, iN THE NEW YORK TiMES

Dejectedly, a man sits on the ground.
The man has been detained. His hands are bound.
His crime is truly simple to explain:
Possessing pictures of Saddam Hussein.
Our soldiers snared him in a swift attack.
They're there to bring our freedoms to Iraq.

—JULY 14, 2003

MEMO

TO: COMMANDER, COALITION FORCES

FROM: KARL ROVE, SUPREME COMMANDER

I now repeat the order that I gave
(And please don't ask again if I am sober):
Replace Saddam Hussein from whence he came,
And capture him again in late October.

—JANUARY 5, 2004

ABOUT THE AUTHOR

Since 1990, Calvin Trillin has been *The Nation*'s "deadline poet," contributing a piece of verse on the news every week. In discussing his political sympathies, he has said, "I am partial to politicians with iambic names that rhyme with a lot of disparaging words."

ABOUT THE TYPE

This book was set in Univers, a typeface created by
Adrian Frutiger at the Paris typefoundry Deberny et
Peignot. This typeface represents a particular achieve-
ment for the designer, who wished to create an orderly
system for delineating type weights and widths, and
sought to creat sans serif characters that were not
solely geometric but had an inviting effect.